SLOW COOKER DOG FOOD COOKBOOK FOR GERMAN SHEPHERDS

Dr. Wesley Glasgow

TABLE OF CONTENTS

INTRODUCTION

My journey into the realm of canine nutrition began decades ago, ignited by an unyielding love for our four-legged companions. It all started with a wagging tail, a wet nose, and a pair of soulful eyes staring up at me—my first dog, Dan. From the moment my parents brought him home when I was just a child, I was captivated by his unwavering loyalty and boundless affection.

Dan wasn't just a pet; he was my confidant, my playmate, and my constant companion. We shared countless adventures, from exploring the backyard to embarking on long walks through the neighbourhood. And amidst it all, there was one thing that brought us even closer together: food.

Like many dog owners, I believed that showering Dan with treats and table scraps was a way to show him love. His pleading eyes and eager tail wagging were impossible to resist, and I found myself indulging his every whim, regardless of the consequences. Little did I know, those innocent gestures of affection would lead to a journey filled with challenges and revelations.

As the years passed, I watched Dan grow older and noticed subtle changes in his behaviour and health. His once boundless energy began to wane, replaced by lethargy and fatigue. His coat lost its lustre, and he started gaining weight at an alarming rate. Concerned for his well-being, I took him to the vet, hoping for answers to the mystery that was unfolding before my eyes.

The diagnosis was devastating Dan had developed diabetes, a condition directly linked to his poor diet and excessive weight gain. My heart sank as I realized that my well-intentioned acts of love had unwittingly put his health at risk. Guilt-ridden and desperate to make amends, I vowed to do everything in my power to help him recover and live the happy, healthy life he deserved.

Under the guidance of our veterinarian, Dan's diet underwent a radical transformation. Gone were the days of indulgence and excess; in their place came a regimen of carefully portioned meals, balanced nutrients, and wholesome ingredients. It was a steep learning curve, filled with trial and error, but the results were nothing short of miraculous.

As Dan's health began to improve, so too did my understanding of the profound impact that nutrition has on our dogs' lives. I delved deep into the science of canine nutrition, devouring books, attending seminars, and seeking out experts in the field. Armed with knowledge and fuelled by passion, I embarked on a quest to find the perfect diet for dogs like Dan—a diet that would nourish their bodies, minds, and spirits from the inside out.

Fast forward 25 years, and I stand before you not only as a devoted dog owner but also as a trained veterinarian specializing in pet nutrition. My journey from a well-meaning dog lover to a seasoned expert in the field has been marked by triumphs and setbacks, but through it all, one thing has remained constant: my unwavering commitment to improving the lives of dogs through the power of nutrition.

Today, as I write these words, I am filled with a sense of purpose and excitement. I am thrilled to share with you the culmination of years of research, experimentation, and passion—a collection of slow cooker recipes tailored specifically to meet the nutritional needs of German Shepherds. But this book is more than just a collection of recipes; it is a testament to the transformative power of good nutrition and the profound bond that exists between dogs and their owners.

In the pages that follow, you'll discover a treasure trove of delicious and nutritious meals designed to nourish your German Shepherd from the inside out. From hearty stews to flavourful treats, each recipe has been meticulously crafted and rigorously tested to ensure optimal health and well-being for your beloved canine companion.

But this book is not just about feeding your dog—it's about nourishing their body, mind, and spirit. Throughout these pages, you'll find valuable insights into the benefits of healthy eating for dogs, as well as the dangers and consequences of a poor diet. You'll learn how to navigate the maze of pet food labels, decipher confusing ingredient lists, and make informed choices about what to feed your furry friend.

So join me on this journey to better nutrition for your German Shepherd. Let's embark on a culinary adventure together, exploring new Flavors, trying new recipes, and uncovering the secrets to a long, happy, and healthy life for our beloved canine companions. Together, we can unleash the full potential of our dogs and celebrate the incredible bond that exists between humans and their faithful companions.

Contact the Author

Thank you for reading my book! I would love to hear from you, whether you have feedback, questions, or just want to share your thoughts. Your feedback means a lot to me and helps me improve as a writer.

Please don't hesitate to reach out to me through

glasgowesley@gmail.com

I look forward to connecting with my readers and appreciate your support in this literary journey. Your thoughts and comments are valuable to me.

CHAPTER 1

Understanding the Importance of Proper Nutrition for German Shepherds

German Shepherds are renowned for their intelligence, loyalty, and athleticism, making them one of the most beloved dog breeds worldwide. However, to maintain their health and vitality, adequate nutrition is paramount. Understanding the importance of proper nutrition for German Shepherds, as well as the benefits of homemade dog food and utilizing a slow cooker for their meals, can significantly contribute to their well-being.

Understanding the Importance of Proper Nutrition for German Shepherds:

German Shepherds have specific dietary needs due to their size, energy levels, and predisposition to certain health issues. Providing them with balanced nutrition ensures they receive essential nutrients for optimal growth, muscle development, and overall health. Proper nutrition also plays a crucial role in supporting their immune system, promoting healthy digestion, and maintaining a shiny coat and strong bones.

A well-rounded diet for German Shepherds typically consists of high-quality protein sources, such as lean meats (e.g., chicken, beef, or fish), complex carbohydrates (e.g., brown rice, sweet potatoes), healthy fats, vitamins, and minerals. It's essential to avoid fillers, artificial additives, and excessive amounts of grains, which may lead to digestive issues or allergies in some dogs.

Benefits of Homemade Dog Food:

Homemade dog food offers several advantages over commercial options. Firstly, it allows pet owners to have full control over the ingredients, ensuring freshness and quality. By preparing meals at home, you can tailor the recipes to meet your German Shepherd's specific dietary requirements and preferences, catering to any food sensitivities or allergies they may have.

Additionally, homemade dog food can be more cost-effective in the long run, especially when buying ingredients in bulk or utilizing leftovers from your own meals. This approach also minimizes the risk of consuming potentially harmful additives or preservatives commonly found in commercial dog food.

Moreover, preparing homemade meals fosters a deeper bond between you and your German Shepherd, as you're actively involved in their care and well-being. It can be a rewarding experience to see your furry friend enjoy nutritious, homemade meals made with love.

Using a Slow Cooker for Dog Food: Why It Works:

Utilizing a slow cooker (or crockpot) for preparing dog food offers convenience, efficiency, and nutritional benefits. Slow cooking allows ingredients to simmer at low temperatures for an extended period, resulting in tender, flavourful meals that retain their nutritional value.

One of the main advantages of using a slow cooker is the convenience it offers busy pet owners. Simply add the ingredients, set the cooker to low heat, and let it do the work while you attend to other tasks. This method is particularly beneficial for preparing large batches of dog food, which can be portioned and stored for future use.

Slow cooking also helps break down tough meat Fibers and bones, making them easier for your German Shepherd to digest and absorb nutrients. Additionally, the long cooking time allows Flavors to meld together, creating enticing aromas that are sure to appeal to your dog's senses.

OTHER BOOKS BY THE AUTHOR

INSTANT POT DOG FOOD COOKBOOK

DOG FOOD COOKBOOK FOR PICKY EATERS

AIR FRYER DOG FOOD COOKBOOK

SLOW COOKER DOG FOOD COOKBOOK

DOG FOOD COOKBOOK FOR SENSITIVE STOMACH

SCAN THE QR CODE TO SEE MORE BOOKS BY AUTHOR

CHAPTER 2
Getting Started

Transitioning to homemade dog food for your German Shepherd is a rewarding endeavor that requires careful planning and preparation. Before embarking on this journey, it's essential to gather the necessary equipment and ingredients, create a meal plan tailored to your dog's needs, and prioritize safety precautions and hygiene practices to ensure the health and well-being of your furry companion.

Equipment and Ingredients:

1. **Equipment:**

   - Large stockpot or slow cooker for cooking

   - Cutting board and sharp knife for chopping ingredients

   - Mixing bowls for combining ingredients

   - Measuring cups and spoons for accurate portioning

   - Food processor or blender for grinding or pureeing

   - Storage containers for storing prepared meals

   - Can opener if using canned ingredients

2. **Ingredients:**

   - High-quality protein sources: Lean meats such as chicken, turkey, beef, or fish.

   - Complex carbohydrates: Brown rice, quinoa, sweet potatoes, or oats.

- Healthy fats: Olive oil, coconut oil, or flaxseed oil.

- Vegetables: Carrots, peas, spinach, broccoli, or pumpkin.

- Fruits: Apples, berries, bananas, or oranges (in moderation).

- Supplements: Consult your veterinarian for recommendations on essential vitamins and minerals to ensure balanced nutrition.

Meal Planning for Your German Shepherd:

1. **Consultation with a Veterinarian:**

   - Before starting a homemade dog food regimen, consult with your veterinarian to determine your German Shepherd's specific dietary requirements, including portion sizes and nutritional needs based on factors such as age, weight, activity level, and any existing health conditions.

2. **Balanced Diet:**

   - Design a meal plan that incorporates a balance of protein, carbohydrates, fats, vitamins, and minerals to meet your dog's nutritional needs. Rotate protein sources and vary ingredients to provide a diverse array of nutrients.

3. **Portion Control:**

   - Calculate the appropriate portion sizes based on your German Shepherd's size and activity level. Monitor their weight and adjust portions as needed to maintain a healthy body condition.

4. **Meal Frequency:**

- Typically, adult German Shepherds require two meals per day, while puppies may need three to four smaller meals. Consult with your veterinarian for guidance on feeding frequency and portion sizes.

Safety Precautions and Hygiene Practices:

1. **Food Handling Safety:**

   - Wash your hands thoroughly before and after handling raw ingredients to prevent the spread of bacteria.

   - Keep raw meat separate from other ingredients to avoid cross-contamination.

   - Thoroughly clean and disinfect all utensils, surfaces, and food preparation areas before and after use.

2. **Cooking and Storage:**

   - Cook meat thoroughly to kill any harmful bacteria. Use a food thermometer to ensure internal temperatures reach safe levels.

   - Divide prepared meals into portion-sized containers and refrigerate or freeze promptly to prevent spoilage.

   - Label containers with the date and contents for easy identification and rotation.

3. **Monitor for Allergies and Reactions:**

   - Introduce new ingredients gradually and monitor your German Shepherd for any signs of allergic reactions or digestive upset.

- Consult with your veterinarian if you suspect food allergies or intolerances and make necessary adjustments to their diet.

By following these guidelines for equipment and ingredients, meal planning, and safety precautions, you can confidently embark on the journey of preparing homemade dog food for your beloved German Shepherd, providing them with nutritious and delicious meals tailored to their specific needs.

CHAPTER 3
Breakfast and Brunch Ideas

Chicken and Sweet Potato Hash

Cooking Time: 6-8 hours on low or 3-4 hours on high

Servings: 4

Ingredients:

- 2 boneless, skinless chicken breasts, diced

- 2 sweet potatoes, peeled and diced

- 1 cup green peas

- 1 cup diced carrots

- 2 cups low-sodium chicken broth

Instructions:

1. Place diced chicken, sweet potatoes, peas, and carrots into the slow cooker.

2. Pour chicken broth over the ingredients.

3. Cook on low for 6-8 hours or on high for 3-4 hours until chicken is cooked through and vegetables are tender.

4. Once cooked, mash ingredients slightly for easier digestion.

5. Serve in appropriate portions for your German Shepherd.

Nutritional Information: Calories: 250, Protein: 20g, Carbohydrates: 30g, Fat: 5g

Beef and Veggie Omelette

Cooking Time: 4-6 hours on low or 2-3 hours on high

Servings: 6

Ingredients:

- 1 lb lean ground beef

- 6 eggs

- 1 cup diced bell peppers

- 1 cup diced zucchini

- 1 cup diced tomatoes

Instructions:

1. Brown ground beef in a skillet over medium heat until cooked through.

2. In a mixing bowl, beat eggs and stir in diced bell peppers, zucchini, and tomatoes.

3. Transfer cooked ground beef and egg mixture to the slow cooker.

4. Cook on low for 4-6 hours or on high for 2-3 hours until eggs are set.

5. Allow to cool slightly before serving to your German Shepherd.

Nutritional Information: Calories: 280, Protein: 25g, Carbohydrates: 10g, Fat: 15g

Turkey and Pumpkin Porridge

Cooking Time: 6-8 hours on low or 3-4 hours on high

Servings: 4

Ingredients:

- 1 lb ground turkey

- 1 cup canned pumpkin puree

- 1 cup rolled oats

- 4 cups water or low-sodium chicken broth

Instructions:

1. In the slow cooker, combine ground turkey, pumpkin puree, rolled oats, and water or broth.

2. Stir well to combine all ingredients.

3. Cook on low for 6-8 hours or on high for 3-4 hours until oats are cooked through and mixture is thickened.

4. Allow to cool before serving to your German Shepherd.

Nutritional Information: Calories: 220, Protein: 18g, Carbohydrates: 15g, Fat: 8g

Salmon and Spinach Scramble

Cooking Time: 4-6 hours on low or 2-3 hours on high

Servings: 6

Ingredients:

- 2 cans (14 oz each) canned salmon, drained

- 2 cups fresh spinach leaves

- 6 eggs

- 1 cup diced mushrooms

Instructions:

1. In a skillet, sauté diced mushrooms until softened.

2. In the slow cooker, combine canned salmon, fresh spinach leaves, sautéed mushrooms, and beaten eggs.

3. Mix well to incorporate all ingredients.

4. Cook on low for 4-6 hours or on high for 2-3 hours until eggs are set.

5. Allow to cool slightly before serving to your German Shepherd.

Nutritional Information: Calories: 240, Protein: 25g, Carbohydrates: 8g, Fat: 12g

Turkey and Vegetable Frittata

Cooking Time: 4-6 hours on low or 2-3 hours on high

Servings: 6

Ingredients:

- 1 lb ground turkey

- 6 eggs

- 1 cup diced broccoli florets

- 1 cup diced bell peppers

- 1 cup diced tomatoes

Instructions:

1. Brown ground turkey in a skillet over medium heat until cooked through.

2. In a mixing bowl, beat eggs and stir in diced broccoli, bell peppers, and tomatoes.

3. Transfer cooked ground turkey and egg mixture to the slow cooker.

4. Cook on low for 4-6 hours or on high for 2-3 hours until eggs are set.

5. Allow to cool slightly before serving to your German Shepherd.

Nutritional Information: Calories: 260, Protein: 22g, Carbohydrates: 10g, Fat: 14g

Chicken and Vegetable Breakfast Bowl

Cooking Time: 6-8 hours on low or 3-4 hours on high

Servings: 4

Ingredients:

- 2 boneless, skinless chicken thighs, diced

- 1 cup diced sweet potatoes

- 1 cup diced zucchini

- 1 cup diced bell peppers

- 1 cup diced carrots

- 2 cups low-sodium chicken broth

Instructions:

1. Place diced chicken thighs, sweet potatoes, zucchini, bell peppers, and carrots into the slow cooker.

2. Pour chicken broth over the ingredients.

3. Cook on low for 6-8 hours or on high for 3-4 hours until chicken is cooked through and vegetables are tender.

4. Once cooked, mash ingredients slightly for easier digestion.

5. Serve in appropriate portions for your German Shepherd.

Nutritional Information: Calories: 240, Protein: 18g, Carbohydrates: 20g, Fat: 10g

Beef and Potato Breakfast Casserole

Cooking Time: 6-8 hours on low or 3-4 hours on high

Servings: 6

Ingredients:

- 1 lb lean ground beef

- 4 cups diced potatoes

- 1 cup diced onions

- 1 cup diced bell peppers

- 1 cup low-sodium beef broth

Instructions:

1. Brown ground beef in a skillet over medium heat until cooked through.

2. In the slow cooker, layer diced potatoes, onions, bell peppers, and cooked ground beef.

3. Pour beef broth over the ingredients.

4. Cook on low for 6-8 hours or on high for 3-4 hours until potatoes are tender.

5. Allow to cool slightly before serving to your German Shepherd.

Nutritional Information: Calories: 280, Protein: 24g, Carbohydrates: 25g, Fat: 10g

Turkey and Quinoa Breakfast Bowl

Cooking Time: 6-8 hours on low or 3-4 hours on high

Servings: 4

Ingredients:

- 1 lb ground turkey

- 1 cup quinoa, rinsed

- 1 cup diced carrots

- 1 cup diced zucchini

- 2 cups low-sodium chicken broth

Instructions:

1. Brown ground turkey in a skillet over medium heat until cooked through.

2. In the slow cooker, combine cooked ground turkey, quinoa, diced carrots, zucchini, and chicken broth.

3. Mix well to incorporate all ingredients.

4. Cook on low for 6-8 hours or on high for 3-4 hours until quinoa is cooked through.

5. Once cooked, allow the mixture to cool slightly before serving to your German Shepherd.

Nutritional Information: Calories: 290, Protein: 24g, Carbohydrates: 25g, Fat: 10g

Chicken and Brown Rice Congee

Cooking Time: 6-8 hours on low or 3-4 hours on high

Servings: 4

Ingredients:

- 2 boneless, skinless chicken breasts, shredded

- 1 cup brown rice

- 6 cups low-sodium chicken broth

- 1 cup diced carrots

- 1 cup diced celery

Instructions:

1. Place shredded chicken, brown rice, diced carrots, and celery into the slow cooker.

2. Pour chicken broth over the ingredients.

3. Cook on low for 6-8 hours or on high for 3-4 hours until rice is cooked through and mixture is thickened.

4. Stir occasionally during cooking to prevent rice from sticking to the bottom.

5. Allow to cool before serving to your German Shepherd.

Nutritional Information: Calories: 270, Protein: 22g, Carbohydrates: 30g, Fat: 5g

Vegetable and Egg Casserole

Cooking Time: 4-6 hours on low or 2-3 hours on high

Servings: 6

Ingredients:

- 6 eggs

- 2 cups diced sweet potatoes

- 1 cup diced bell peppers

- 1 cup diced zucchini

- 1 cup diced tomatoes

- 1 cup chopped spinach

Instructions:

1. In a mixing bowl, beat eggs and stir in diced sweet potatoes, bell peppers, zucchini, tomatoes, and chopped spinach.

2. Transfer the mixture to the slow cooker.

3. Cook on low for 4-6 hours or on high for 2-3 hours until eggs are set.

4. Allow to cool slightly before serving to your German Shepherd.

Nutritional Information: Calories: 230, Protein: 18g, Carbohydrates: 15g, Fat: 10g

CHAPTER 4

Nourishing Soups and Stews

Chicken and Vegetable Stew

Cooking Time: 6-8 hours on low or 3-4 hours on high

Servings: 6

Ingredients:

- 2 boneless, skinless chicken breasts, diced

- 2 sweet potatoes, peeled and diced

- 1 cup green beans, chopped

- 1 cup carrots, diced

- 4 cups low-sodium chicken broth

Instructions:

1. Place diced chicken, sweet potatoes, green beans, and carrots into the slow cooker.

2. Pour chicken broth over the ingredients.

3. Cook on low for 6-8 hours or on high for 3-4 hours until chicken is cooked through and vegetables are tender.

4. Once cooked, shred the chicken and mix well.

5. Allow to cool before serving to your German Shepherd.

Nutritional Information: Calories: 220, Protein: 20g, Carbohydrates: 25g, Fat: 5g

Beef and Barley Soup

Cooking Time: 6-8 hours on low or 3-4 hours on high

Servings: 6

Ingredients:

- 1 lb lean stew beef, cubed

- 1 cup barley, rinsed

- 2 cups diced carrots

- 2 cups diced celery

- 1 cup peas

Instructions:

1. Place cubed beef, barley, carrots, celery, and peas into the slow cooker.

2. Add enough water to cover the ingredients.

3. Cook on low for 6-8 hours or on high for 3-4 hours until beef is tender and barley is cooked through.

4. Stir occasionally during cooking.

5. Allow to cool slightly before serving to your German Shepherd.

Nutritional Information: Calories: 250, Protein: 22g, Carbohydrates: 30g, Fat: 6g

Turkey and Pumpkin Stew

Cooking Time: 6-8 hours on low or 3-4 hours on high

Servings: 4

Ingredients:

- 1 lb ground turkey

- 1 cup canned pumpkin puree

- 1 cup brown rice

- 2 cups low-sodium chicken broth

- 1 cup diced carrots

Instructions:

1. Brown ground turkey in a skillet over medium heat until cooked through.

2. In the slow cooker, combine cooked ground turkey, pumpkin puree, brown rice, chicken broth, and diced carrots.

3. Mix well to incorporate all ingredients.

4. Cook on low for 6-8 hours or on high for 3-4 hours until rice is cooked through and stew is thickened.

5. Allow to cool before serving to your German Shepherd.

Nutritional Information: Calories: 240, Protein: 20g, Carbohydrates: 25g, Fat: 7g

Salmon and Potato Chowder

Cooking Time: 4-6 hours on low or 2-3 hours on high

Servings: 4

Ingredients:

- 2 cans (14 oz each) canned salmon, drained
- 2 potatoes, peeled and diced
- 1 cup diced carrots
- 1 cup diced celery
- 4 cups low-sodium vegetable broth

Instructions:

1. In the slow cooker, combine canned salmon, diced potatoes, carrots, celery, and vegetable broth.
2. Mix well to incorporate all ingredients.
3. Cook on low for 4-6 hours or on high for 2-3 hours until potatoes are tender.
4. Once cooked, mash the potatoes slightly to thicken the chowder.
5. Allow to cool slightly before serving to your German Shepherd.

Nutritional Information: Calories: 270, Protein: 24g, Carbohydrates: 20g, Fat: 10g

Chicken and Rice Soup

Cooking Time: 6-8 hours on low or 3-4 hours on high

Servings: 6

Ingredients:

- 2 boneless, skinless chicken thighs, diced

- 1 cup white rice

- 2 cups diced carrots

- 2 cups diced celery

- 4 cups low-sodium chicken broth

Instructions:

1. Place diced chicken thighs, white rice, carrots, and celery into the slow cooker.

2. Pour chicken broth over the ingredients.

3. Cook on low for 6-8 hours or on high for 3-4 hours until chicken is cooked through and rice is tender.

4. Once cooked, shred the chicken and mix well.

5. Allow to cool before serving to your German Shepherd.

Nutritional Information: Calories: 250, Protein: 22g, Carbohydrates: 30g, Fat: 6g

Beef and Vegetable Stew

Cooking Time: 6-8 hours on low or 3-4 hours on high

Servings: 6

Ingredients:

- 1 lb stew beef, cubed

- 2 potatoes, peeled and diced

- 2 cups diced carrots

- 2 cups diced celery

- 4 cups low-sodium beef broth

Instructions:

1. Place cubed beef, potatoes, carrots, and celery into the slow cooker.

2. Pour beef broth over the ingredients.

3. Cook on low for 6-8 hours or on high for 3-4 hours until beef is tender and vegetables are cooked through.

4. Stir occasionally during cooking.

5. Allow to cool slightly before serving to your German Shepherd.

Nutritional Information: Calories: 280, Protein: 24g, Carbohydrates: 25g, Fat: 8g

Turkey and Lentil Soup

Cooking Time: 6-8 hours on low or 3-4 hours on high

Servings: 4

Ingredients:

- 1 lb ground turkey

- 1 cup dried lentils, rinsed

- 2 cups diced sweet potatoes

- 2 cups diced tomatoes

- 4 cups low-sodium chicken broth

Instructions:

1. Brown ground turkey in a skillet over medium heat until cooked through.

2. In the slow cooker, combine cooked ground turkey, lentils, sweet potatoes, tomatoes, and chicken broth.

3. Mix well to incorporate all ingredients.

4. Cook on low for 6-8 hours or on high for 3-4 hours until lentils are tender and soup is thickened.

5. Allow to cool before serving to your German Shepherd.

Nutritional Information: Calories: 240, Protein: 20g, Carbohydrates: 25g, Fat: 7g

Chicken and Quinoa Stew

Cooking Time: 6-8 hours on low or 3-4 hours on high

Servings: 4

Ingredients:

- 2 boneless, skinless chicken breasts, diced

- 1 cup quinoa, rinsed

- 2 cups diced carrots

- 2 cups diced zucchini

- 4 cups low-sodium chicken broth

Instructions:

1. Place diced chicken breasts, quinoa, carrots, and zucchini into the slow cooker.

2. Pour chicken broth over the ingredients.

3. Cook on low for 6-8 hours or on high for 3-4 hours until chicken is cooked through and quinoa is tender.

4. Once cooked, allow to cool before serving to your German Shepherd.

Nutritional Information: Calories: 230, Protein: 20g, Carbohydrates: 25g, Fat: 5g

Salmon and Vegetable Chowder

Cooking Time: 4-6 hours on low or 2-3 hours on high

Servings: 4

Ingredients:

- 2 cans (14 oz each) canned salmon, drained

- 2 potatoes, peeled and diced

- 1 cup diced carrots

- 1 cup diced celery

- 4 cups low-sodium vegetable broth

Instructions:

1. In the slow cooker, combine canned salmon, diced potatoes, carrots, celery, and vegetable broth.

2. Mix well to incorporate all ingredients.

3. Cook on low for 4-6 hours or on high for 2-3 hours until potatoes are tender.

4. Once cooked, mash the potatoes slightly to thicken the chowder.

5. Allow to cool slightly before serving to your German Shepherd.

Nutritional Information: Calories: 270, Protein: 24g, Carbohydrates: 20g, Fat: 10g

Turkey and Rice Congee

Cooking Time: 6-8 hours on low or 3-4 hours on high

Servings: 4

Ingredients:

- 1 lb ground turkey
- 1 cup white rice
- 4 cups low-sodium chicken broth
- 1 cup diced carrots
- 1 cup diced celery

Instructions:

1. Brown ground turkey in a skillet over medium heat until cooked through.
2. In the slow cooker, combine cooked ground turkey, white rice, chicken broth, carrots, and celery.
3. Mix well to incorporate all ingredients.
4. Cook on low for 6-8 hours or on high for 3-4 hours until rice is cooked through and congee is thickened.
5. Allow to cool before serving to your German Shepherd.

Nutritional Information: Calories: 240, Protein: 20g, Carbohydrates: 25g, Fat: 7g

CHAPTER 5

Wholesome Main Courses

Beef and Vegetable Casserole

Cooking Time: 6-8 hours on low or 3-4 hours on high

Servings: 6

Ingredients:

- 1 lb lean beef stew meat, cubed

- 2 potatoes, peeled and diced

- 1 cup diced carrots

- 1 cup diced celery

- 1 cup diced bell peppers

- 2 cups low-sodium beef broth

Instructions:

1. Place cubed beef, potatoes, carrots, celery, and bell peppers into the slow cooker.

2. Pour beef broth over the ingredients.

3. Mix well to combine.

4. Cook on low for 6-8 hours or on high for 3-4 hours until beef is tender and vegetables are cooked through.

5. Allow to cool before serving to your German Shepherd.

Nutritional Information: Calories: 270, Protein: 24g, Carbohydrates: 25g, Fat: 8g

Turkey and Brown Rice Casserole

Cooking Time: 6-8 hours on low or 3-4 hours on high

Servings: 4

Ingredients:

- 1 lb ground turkey

- 1 cup brown rice

- 2 cups diced sweet potatoes

- 1 cup diced carrots

- 4 cups low-sodium chicken broth

Instructions:

1. Brown ground turkey in a skillet over medium heat until cooked through.

2. In the slow cooker, combine cooked ground turkey, brown rice, sweet potatoes, carrots, and chicken broth.

3. Mix well to combine.

4. Cook on low for 6-8 hours or on high for 3-4 hours until rice is tender and casserole is heated through.

5. Allow to cool slightly before serving to your German Shepherd.

Nutritional Information: Calories: 240, Protein: 20g, Carbohydrates: 25g, Fat: 7g

Chicken and Vegetable Stew

Cooking Time: 6-8 hours on low or 3-4 hours on high

Servings: 6

Ingredients:

- 2 boneless, skinless chicken breasts, diced

- 2 potatoes, peeled and diced

- 1 cup diced carrots

- 1 cup diced celery

- 1 cup green beans, chopped

- 4 cups low-sodium chicken broth

Instructions:

1. Place diced chicken, potatoes, carrots, celery, and green beans into the slow cooker.

2. Pour chicken broth over the ingredients.

3. Mix well to combine.

4. Cook on low for 6-8 hours or on high for 3-4 hours until chicken is cooked through and vegetables are tender.

5. Allow to cool before serving to your German Shepherd.

Nutritional Information: Calories: 250, Protein: 22g, Carbohydrates: 30g, Fat: 6g

Salmon and Quinoa Pilaf

Cooking Time: 4-6 hours on low or 2-3 hours on high

Servings: 4

Ingredients:

- 2 cans (14 oz each) canned salmon, drained

- 1 cup quinoa, rinsed

- 2 cups diced sweet potatoes

- 1 cup diced zucchini

- 4 cups low-sodium vegetable broth

Instructions:

1. In the slow cooker, combine canned salmon, quinoa, sweet potatoes, zucchini, and vegetable broth.

2. Mix well to combine.

3. Cook on low for 4-6 hours or on high for 2-3 hours until quinoa is cooked through and vegetables are tender.

4. Allow to cool slightly before serving to your German Shepherd.

Nutritional Information: Calories: 270, Protein: 24g, Carbohydrates: 25g, Fat: 9g

Beef and Lentil Stew

Cooking Time: 6-8 hours on low or 3-4 hours on high

Servings: 6

Ingredients:

- 1 lb beef stew meat, cubed

- 1 cup dried lentils, rinsed

- 2 cups diced potatoes

- 1 cup diced carrots

- 1 cup diced onions

- 4 cups low-sodium beef broth

Instructions:

1. Place cubed beef, lentils, potatoes, carrots, and onions into the slow cooker.

2. Pour beef broth over the ingredients.

3. Mix well to combine.

4. Cook on low for 6-8 hours or on high for 3-4 hours until beef is tender and lentils are cooked through.

5. Allow to cool before serving to your German Shepherd.

Nutritional Information: Calories: 280, Protein: 26g, Carbohydrates: 25g, Fat: 8g

Turkey and Vegetable Stir-Fry

Cooking Time: 4-6 hours on low or 2-3 hours on high

Servings: 4

Ingredients:

- 1 lb ground turkey
- 2 cups diced bell peppers (assorted colors)
- 2 cups diced zucchini
- 1 cup diced carrots
- 1 cup diced broccoli florets
- 1/4 cup low-sodium soy sauce

Instructions:

1. Brown ground turkey in a skillet over medium heat until cooked through.
2. In the slow cooker, combine cooked ground turkey, diced bell peppers, zucchini, carrots, and broccoli.
3. Drizzle soy sauce over the ingredients.
4. Mix well to combine.
5. Cook on low for 4-6 hours or on high for 2-3 hours until vegetables are tender.
6. Allow to cool slightly before serving to your German Shepherd.

Nutritional Information: Calories: 240, Protein: 22g, Carbohydrates: 20g, Fat: 8g

Chicken and Rice Pilaf

Cooking Time: 6-8 hours on low or 3-4 hours on high

Servings: 6

Ingredients:

- 2 boneless, skinless chicken breasts, diced

- 1 cup white rice

- 2 cups diced carrots

- 2 cups diced celery

- 4 cups low-sodium chicken broth

Instructions:

1. Place diced chicken breasts, rice, carrots, and celery into the slow cooker.

2. Pour chicken broth over the ingredients.

3. Mix well to combine.

4. Cook on low for 6-8 hours or on high for 3-4 hours until chicken is cooked through and rice is tender.

5. Allow to cool before serving to your German Shepherd.

Nutritional Information: Calories: 250, Protein: 22g, Carbohydrates: 30g, Fat: 6g

Beef and Vegetable Stir-Fry

Cooking Time: 4-6 hours on low or 2-3 hours on high

Servings: 4

Ingredients:

- 1 lb lean beef steak, thinly sliced

- 2 cups sliced mushrooms

- 2 cups sliced bell peppers (assorted colors)

- 1 cup sliced onions

- 1 cup snow peas

- 1/4 cup low-sodium soy sauce

Instructions:

1. In the slow cooker, combine sliced beef steak, mushrooms, bell peppers, onions, and snow peas.

2. Drizzle soy sauce over the ingredients.

3. Mix well to combine.

4. Cook on low for 4-6 hours or on high for 2-3 hours until beef is tender.

5. Allow to cool slightly before serving to your German Shepherd.

Nutritional Information: Calories: 280, Protein: 26g, Carbohydrates: 15g, Fat: 10g

Turkey and Vegetable Casserole

Cooking Time: 6-8 hours on low or 3-4 hours on high

Servings: 6

Ingredients:

- 1 lb ground turkey

- 2 cups diced sweet potatoes

- 2 cups diced zucchini

- 1 cup diced carrots

- 1 cup diced onions

- 4 cups low-sodium chicken broth

Instructions:

1. Brown ground turkey in a skillet over medium heat until cooked through.

2. In the slow cooker, combine cooked ground turkey, sweet potatoes, zucchini, carrots, onions, and chicken broth.

3. Mix well to combine.

4. Cook on low for 6-8 hours or on high for 3-4 hours until vegetables are tender.

5. Allow to cool before serving to your German Shepherd.

Nutritional Information: Calories: 240, Protein: 20g, Carbohydrates: 25g, Fat: 7g

Salmon and Sweet Potato Bake

Cooking Time: 4-6 hours on low or 2-3 hours on high

Servings: 4

Ingredients:

- 2 cans (14 oz each) canned salmon, drained

- 2 sweet potatoes, peeled and sliced

- 1 cup diced tomatoes

- 1 cup diced bell peppers

- 1/4 cup olive oil

Instructions:

1. In the slow cooker, layer slices of sweet potatoes, canned salmon, diced tomatoes, and diced bell peppers.

2. Drizzle olive oil over the ingredients.

3. Repeat layering until all ingredients are used.

4. Cook on low for 4-6 hours or on high for 2-3 hours until sweet potatoes are tender.

5. Allow to cool slightly before serving to your German Shepherd.

Nutritional Information: Calories: 260, Protein: 24g, Carbohydrates: 20g, Fat: 10g

CHAPTER 6
Delicious Treats and Snacks

Peanut Butter and Banana Bites

Cooking Time: 2 hours on low

Servings: 12 bites

Ingredients:

- 2 ripe bananas, mashed

- 1/2 cup natural peanut butter (make sure it doesn't contain xylitol)

- 1 cup rolled oats

Instructions:

1. In a mixing bowl, combine mashed bananas, peanut butter, and rolled oats.

2. Stir until well combined.

3. Shape the mixture into small bite-sized balls.

4. Place the balls on a greased slow cooker liner.

5. Cook on low for 2 hours.

6. Allow to cool completely before serving to your German Shepherd.

Nutritional Information: Calories: 80, Protein: 3g, Carbohydrates: 10g, Fat: 4g

Apple and Carrot Dog Cookies

Cooking Time: 3 hours on low

Servings: 24 cookies

Ingredients:

- 2 cups grated apples

- 1 cup grated carrots

- 2 cups whole wheat flour

- 1 egg

Instructions:

1. In a mixing bowl, combine grated apples, grated carrots, whole wheat flour, and egg.

2. Mix until a dough forms.

3. Roll out the dough on a floured surface and cut into small cookie shapes.

4. Place the cookies on a greased slow cooker liner.

5. Cook on low for 3 hours.

6. Allow to cool before serving to your German Shepherd.

Nutritional Information: Calories: 45, Protein: 1g, Carbohydrates: 10g, Fat: 0.5g

Chicken and Sweet Potato Jerky

Cooking Time: 4 hours on low

Servings: 10 strips

Ingredients:

- 1 lb boneless, skinless chicken breast, thinly sliced

- 1 sweet potato, peeled and thinly sliced

Instructions:

1. Preheat your slow cooker on low heat.

2. Alternate layers of chicken and sweet potato slices on the bottom of the slow cooker.

3. Cover and cook for 4 hours.

4. Once cooked and dried, allow the jerky to cool completely.

5. Cut into strips.

6. Store in an airtight container in the refrigerator for up to one week.

Nutritional Information: Calories: 70, Protein: 8g, Carbohydrates: 5g, Fat: 1g

Pumpkin and Oatmeal Dog Treats

Cooking Time: 3 hours on low

Servings: 20 treats

Ingredients:

- 1 cup canned pumpkin puree

- 2 cups rolled oats

- 1/4 cup water

Instructions:

1. In a mixing bowl, combine canned pumpkin puree, rolled oats, and water.

2. Mix until a dough forms.

3. Roll out the dough on a floured surface and cut into small treat shapes.

4. Place the treats on a greased slow cooker liner.

5. Cook on low for 3 hours.

6. Allow to cool before serving to your German Shepherd.

Nutritional Information: Calories: 35, Protein: 1g, Carbohydrates: 7g, Fat: 0.5g

Blueberry and Banana Frozen Treats

Preparation Time: 10 minutes

Freezing Time: 4 hours

Servings: 12 treats

Ingredients:

- 2 ripe bananas, mashed

- 1 cup blueberries

- 1 cup plain yogurt (make sure it doesn't contain xylitol)

Instructions:

1. In a blender, combine mashed bananas, blueberries, and yogurt.

2. Blend until smooth.

3. Pour the mixture into ice cube trays or silicone molds.

4. Freeze for at least 4 hours until solid.

5. Pop out the frozen treats and store in a freezer-safe bag or container.

6. Serve frozen as a refreshing treat for your German Shepherd.

Nutritional Information: Calories: 25, Protein: 1g, Carbohydrates: 5g, Fat: 0.5g

Turkey and Cranberry Dog Biscuits

Cooking Time: 3 hours on low

Servings: 24 biscuits

Ingredients:

- 1 cup cooked turkey, diced

- 1/2 cup dried cranberries

- 2 cups whole wheat flour

- 1 egg

- 1/4 cup water

Instructions:

1. In a mixing bowl, combine diced turkey, dried cranberries, whole wheat flour, egg, and water.

2. Mix until a dough forms.

3. Roll out the dough on a floured surface and cut into small biscuit shapes.

4. Place the biscuits on a greased slow cooker liner.

5. Cook on low for 3 hours.

6. Allow to cool before serving to your German Shepherd.

Nutritional Information: Calories: 50, Protein: 3g, Carbohydrates: 7g, Fat: 1g

Carrot and Spinach Dog Muffins

Cooking Time: 3 hours on low

Servings: 12 muffins

Ingredients:

- 2 cups grated carrots

- 1 cup chopped spinach

- 2 cups whole wheat flour

- 1 egg

- 1/4 cup vegetable oil

Instructions:

1. In a mixing bowl, combine grated carrots, chopped spinach, whole wheat flour, egg, and vegetable oil.

2. Mix until a batter forms.

3. Spoon the batter into muffin cups lined with cupcake liners.

4. Place the muffin cups in the slow cooker.

5. Cook on low for 3 hours.

6. Allow to cool before serving to your German Shepherd.

Nutritional Information: Calories: 80, Protein: 2g, Carbohydrates: 10g, Fat: 4g

Chicken Liver and Pumpkin Bites

Cooking Time: 2 hours on low

Servings: 16 bites

Ingredients:

- 1 cup cooked chicken liver, chopped

- 1/2 cup canned pumpkin puree

- 1 cup whole wheat flour

- 1 egg

Instructions:

1. In a mixing bowl, combine chopped chicken liver, pumpkin puree, whole wheat flour, and egg.

2. Mix until well combined.

3. Shape the mixture into small bite-sized balls.

4. Place the balls on a greased slow cooker liner.

5. Cook on low for 2 hours.

6. Allow to cool before serving to your German Shepherd.

Nutritional Information: Calories: 45, Protein: 3g, Carbohydrates: 5g, Fat: 1g

Cheese and Carrot Dog Biscuits

Cooking Time: 3 hours on low

Servings: 24 biscuits

Ingredients:

- 1 cup grated cheese

- 1 cup grated carrots

- 2 cups whole wheat flour

- 1 egg

- 1/4 cup water

Instructions:

1. In a mixing bowl, combine grated cheese, grated carrots, whole wheat flour, egg, and water.

2. Mix until a dough forms.

3. Roll out the dough on a floured surface and cut into small biscuit shapes.

4. Place the biscuits on a greased slow cooker liner.

5. Cook on low for 3 hours.

6. Allow to cool before serving to your German Shepherd.

Nutritional Information: Calories: 50, Protein: 3g, Carbohydrates: 6g, Fat: 2g

Beef and Sweet Potato Dog Jerky

Cooking Time: 4 hours on low

Servings: 12 strips

Ingredients:

- 1 lb lean beef steak, thinly sliced

- 1 sweet potato, peeled and thinly sliced

Instructions:

1. Preheat your slow cooker on low heat.

2. Alternate layers of beef and sweet potato slices on the bottom of the slow cooker.

3. Cover and cook for 4 hours.

4. Once cooked and dried, allow the jerky to cool completely.

5. Cut into strips.

6. Store in an airtight container in the refrigerator for up to one week.

Nutritional Information: Calories: 80, Protein: 6g, Carbohydrates: 5g, Fat: 3g

CHAPTER 7

Special Dietary Considerations Dogs with Specific Needs

Grain-Free Chicken and Vegetable Stew

Cooking Time: 6-8 hours on low or 3-4 hours on high

Servings: 6

Ingredients:

- 2 boneless, skinless chicken breasts, diced
- 2 sweet potatoes, peeled and diced
- 1 cup diced carrots
- 1 cup diced zucchini
- 4 cups low-sodium chicken broth

Instructions:

1. Place diced chicken, sweet potatoes, carrots, and zucchini into the slow cooker.
2. Pour chicken broth over the ingredients.
3. Mix well to combine.
4. Cook on low for 6-8 hours or on high for 3-4 hours until chicken is cooked through and vegetables are tender.
5. Allow to cool before serving to your German Shepherd.

Nutritional Information: Calories: 250, Protein: 22g, Carbohydrates: 30g, Fat: 6g

Sensitive Stomach Turkey and Rice Casserole

Cooking Time: 6-8 hours on low or 3-4 hours on high

Servings: 4

Ingredients:

- 1 lb ground turkey

- 1 cup cooked white rice

- 1 cup canned pumpkin puree

- 1 cup diced carrots

- 4 cups low-sodium chicken broth

Instructions:

1. Brown ground turkey in a skillet over medium heat until cooked through.

2. In the slow cooker, combine cooked ground turkey, cooked white rice, pumpkin puree, carrots, and chicken broth.

3. Mix well to combine.

4. Cook on low for 6-8 hours or on high for 3-4 hours until casserole is heated through.

5. Allow to cool slightly before serving to your German Shepherd.

Nutritional Information: Calories: 230, Protein: 20g, Carbohydrates: 25g, Fat: 7g

Weight Management Turkey and Vegetable Stew

Cooking Time: 6-8 hours on low or 3-4 hours on high

Servings: 6

Ingredients:

- 1 lb ground turkey

- 2 cups diced sweet potatoes

- 2 cups diced carrots

- 2 cups diced green beans

- 4 cups low-sodium chicken broth

Instructions:

1. Brown ground turkey in a skillet over medium heat until cooked through.

2. In the slow cooker, combine cooked ground turkey, sweet potatoes, carrots, grccn bcans, and chickcn broth.

3. Mix well to combine.

4. Cook on low for 6-8 hours or on high for 3-4 hours until vegetables are tender.

5. Allow to cool before serving to your German Shepherd.

Nutritional Information: Calories: 240, Protein: 20g, Carbohydrates: 25g, Fat: 7g

Limited Ingredient Diet Lamb and Potato Stew

Cooking Time: 6-8 hours on low or 3-4 hours on high

Servings: 4

Ingredients:

- 1 lb lean lamb meat, cubed

- 2 potatoes, peeled and diced

- 1 cup diced carrots

- 1 cup diced green beans

- 4 cups low-sodium lamb broth

Instructions:

1. Place cubed lamb meat, potatoes, carrots, and green beans into the slow cooker.

2. Pour lamb broth over the ingredients.

3. Mix well to combine.

4. Cook on low for 6-8 hours or on high for 3-4 hours until lamb is tender and vegetables are cooked through.

5. Allow to cool before serving to your German Shepherd.

Nutritional Information: Calories: 270, Protein: 24g, Carbohydrates: 25g, Fat: 8g

Digestive Health Chicken and Pumpkin Soup

Cooking Time: 6-8 hours on low or 3-4 hours on high

Servings: 6

Ingredients:

- 2 boneless, skinless chicken breasts, diced

- 1 cup cooked brown rice

- 1 cup canned pumpkin puree

- 1 cup diced carrots

- 4 cups low-sodium chicken broth

Instructions:

1. Place diced chicken, cooked brown rice, pumpkin puree, and carrots into the slow cooker.

2. Pour chicken broth over the ingredients.

3. Mix well to combine.

4. Cook on low for 6-8 hours or on high for 3-4 hours until chicken is cooked through and soup is heated through.

5. Allow to cool before serving to your German Shepherd.

Nutritional Information: Calories: 240, Protein: 22g, Carbohydrates: 30g, Fat: 6g

Joint Health Beef and Sweet Potato Stew

Cooking Time: 6-8 hours on low or 3-4 hours on high

Servings: 4

Ingredients:

- 1 lb beef stew meat, cubed

- 2 sweet potatoes, peeled and diced

- 1 cup diced carrots

- 1 cup diced green beans

- 4 cups low-sodium beef broth

Instructions:

1. Place cubed beef, sweet potatoes, carrots, and green beans into the slow cooker.

2. Pour beef broth over the ingredients.

3. Mix well to combine.

4. Cook on low for 6-8 hours or on high for 3-4 hours until beef is tender and vegetables are cooked through.

5. Allow to cool before serving to your German Shepherd.

Nutritional Information: Calories: 270, Protein: 24g, Carbohydrates: 25g, Fat: 8g

Senior Dog Turkey and Rice Casserole

Cooking Time: 6-8 hours on low or 3-4 hours on high

Servings: 4

Ingredients:

- 1 lb ground turkey

- 1 cup cooked brown rice

- 1 cup diced sweet potatoes

- 1 cup diced carrots

- 4 cups low-sodium chicken broth

Instructions:

1. Brown ground turkey in a skillet over medium heat until cooked through.

2. In the slow cooker, combine cooked ground turkey, cooked brown rice, sweet potatoes, carrots, and chicken broth.

3. Mix well to combine.

4. Cook on low for 6-8 hours or on high for 3-4 hours until casserole is heated through.

5. Allow to cool slightly before serving to your senior German Shepherd.

Nutritional Information: Calories: 240, Protein: 20g, Carbohydrates: 25g, Fat: 7g

Allergy-Friendly Salmon and Potato Chowder

Cooking Time: 4-6 hours on low or 2-3 hours on high

Servings: 4

Ingredients:

- 2 cans (14 oz each) canned salmon, drained

- 2 potatoes, peeled and diced

- 1 cup diced carrots

- 1 cup diced celery

- 4 cups low-sodium vegetable broth

Instructions:

1. In the slow cooker, combine canned salmon, diced potatoes, carrots, celery, and vegetable broth.

2. Mix well to incorporate all ingredients.

3. Cook on low for 4-6 hours or on high for 2-3 hours until potatoes are tender.

4. Once cooked, mash the potatoes slightly to thicken the chowder.

5. Allow to cool slightly before serving to your German Shepherd with allergies.

Nutritional Information: Calories: 270, Protein: 24g, Carbohydrates: 20g, Fat: 10g

Low-Fat Chicken and Rice Soup

Cooking Time: 6-8 hours on low or 3-4 hours on high

Servings: 6

Ingredients:

- 2 boneless, skinless chicken breasts, diced

- 1 cup cooked white rice

- 2 cups diced carrots

- 2 cups diced celery

- 4 cups low-sodium chicken broth

Instructions:

1. Place diced chicken, cooked white rice, carrots, and celery into the slow cooker.

2. Pour chicken broth over the ingredients.

3. Mix well to combine.

4. Cook on low for 6-8 hours or on high for 3-4 hours until chicken is cooked through and soup is heated through.

5. Allow to cool before serving to your German Shepherd.

Nutritional Information: Calories: 250, Protein: 22g, Carbohydrates: 30g, Fat: 6g

Digestive Support Turkey and Pumpkin Stew

Cooking Time: 6-8 hours on low or 3-4 hours on high

Servings: 6

Ingredients:

- 1 lb ground turkey

- 1 cup canned pumpkin puree

- 2 cups diced sweet potatoes

- 1 cup diced carrots

- 4 cups low-sodium chicken broth

Instructions:

1. Brown ground turkey in a skillet over medium heat until cooked through.

2. In the slow cooker, combine cooked ground turkey, pumpkin puree, sweet potatoes, carrots, and chicken broth.

3. Mix well to combine.

4. Cook on low for 6-8 hours or on high for 3-4 hours until vegetables are tender.

5. Allow to cool before serving to your German Shepherd.

Nutritional Information: Calories: 240, Protein: 20g, Carbohydrates: 25g, Fat: 7g

CONCLUSION

As we reach the end of this culinary journey tailored to German Shepherds, I am filled with gratitude for the opportunity to share my passion for canine nutrition with you. Throughout this book, we've explored the transformative power of wholesome ingredients, delicious flavors, and nourishing meals, all designed to support the health and well-being of our beloved furry friends.

But our journey doesn't end here. As you embark on your own adventures in the kitchen, I encourage you to embrace experimentation, creativity, and curiosity. Don't be afraid to tweak recipes to suit your dog's preferences and dietary needs, and always prioritize their health and happiness above all else.

Your feedback is invaluable to me as I continue to refine and improve my recipes and techniques. Whether you found a particular recipe to be a hit with your German Shepherd or have suggestions for how I can enhance future editions of this cookbook, I welcome your input with open arms.

In addition, I encourage you to leave an honest review of this book on whichever platform you purchased it from. Your reviews not only help other dog owners discover the benefits of slow cooker dog food tailored to German Shepherds but also provide valuable insights for me as I strive to better serve the needs of our canine companions.

Together, let's continue to nourish our German Shepherds with love, care, and nutritious meals, ensuring that they lead happy, healthy, and fulfilling lives by our sides.

Thank you for joining me on this journey, and may your kitchen be filled with wagging tails, slobbery kisses, and the joyous barks of contented dogs.

BONUS 1
Training Tips for German Shepherds

German Shepherds are renowned for their intelligence, loyalty, and versatility, making them one of the most trainable breeds. With the right approach and consistency, you can unlock your German Shepherd's full potential and cultivate a strong bond built on mutual respect and understanding. In this chapter, we'll explore effective training techniques tailored specifically to German Shepherds, covering obedience training, socialization, and addressing common behavioural challenges.

1. Start Early: Begin training your German Shepherd as soon as you bring them home, ideally when they are still puppies. Early socialization and basic obedience training lay the foundation for a well-behaved and well-adjusted adult dog.

2. Positive Reinforcement: German Shepherds respond exceptionally well to positive reinforcement training methods. Use treats, praise, and rewards to encourage desired behaviours such as sitting, staying, and walking politely on a leash. Avoid harsh punishments or physical corrections, as these can damage the trust between you and your dog.

3. Consistency is Key: Consistency is crucial in training a German Shepherd. Use clear and consistent commands and enforce rules consistently to avoid confusion. Establish a routine for training sessions and stick to it, keeping sessions short and engaging to maintain your dog's focus and motivation.

4. Leadership Role: German Shepherds have a strong pack mentality and thrive in environments where they understand their place in the hierarchy. Establish yourself as the leader through calm, assertive leadership, and provide clear direction and guidance to your dog. Consistent leadership helps prevent behavioural issues such as dominance and aggression.

5. Socialization: Expose your German Shepherd to various environments, people, animals, and experiences from an early age to ensure they grow up to be well-adjusted and confident adults. Organize playdates with other friendly dogs, introduce them to different sights and sounds, and provide positive interactions with people of all ages and backgrounds.

6. Mental Stimulation: German Shepherds are highly intelligent and require mental stimulation to prevent boredom and destructive behaviours. Incorporate brain games, puzzle toys, and training exercises that challenge their problem-solving skills and keep them mentally sharp.

7. Leash Training: Teach your German Shepherd to walk politely on a leash using positive reinforcement techniques. Start in a quiet, distraction-free environment and gradually introduce distractions as your dog becomes more proficient. Use treats and praise to reward loose leash walking and discourage pulling.

8. Addressing Behavioural Challenges: If you encounter behavioural challenges such as excessive barking, separation anxiety, or aggression, address them promptly with positive reinforcement training and, if necessary, seek guidance from a professional dog trainer or behaviorist. Patience, consistency, and understanding are key to overcoming behavioural issues.

9. Advanced Training: Once your German Shepherd has mastered basic obedience commands, consider enrolling them in advanced training classes such as agility, obedience trials, or scent work. These activities not only provide mental and physical stimulation but also strengthen the bond between you and your dog.

10. Patience and Persistence: Training a German Shepherd requires patience, persistence, and a deep understanding of the breed's unique characteristics. Celebrate small victories, remain patient during setbacks, and never underestimate the power of consistent training and positive reinforcement in shaping your dog's behaviour and temperament.

BONUS 2
30 Day Meal Plan

Day	Breakfast	Lunch	Dinner	Snacks
1	Peanut Butter and Banana Bites	Chicken and Sweet Potato Stew	Beef and Vegetable Stew	Carrot and Spinach Dog Muffins
2	Apple and Carrot Dog Cookies	Turkey and Vegetable Casserole	Chicken and Rice Pilaf	Blueberry and Banana Frozen Treats
3	Pumpkin and Oatmeal Dog Treats	Salmon and Sweet Potato Bake	Turkey and Cranberry Dog Biscuits	Cheese and Carrot Dog Biscuits
4	Blueberry and Banana Frozen Treats	Beef and Sweet Potato Stew	Chicken and Vegetable Stir-Fry	Peanut Butter and Banana Bites
5	Chicken Liver and Pumpkin Bites	Chicken and Rice Soup	Turkey and Vegetable Stir-Fry	Apple and Carrot Dog Cookies
6	Turkey and Cranberry Dog Biscuits	Turkey and Vegetable Casserole	Beef and Vegetable Stew	Pumpkin and Oatmeal Dog Treats
7	Cheese and Carrot Dog Biscuits	Salmon and Sweet Potato Bake	Chicken and Rice Pilaf	Blueberry and Banana Frozen Treats

8	Carrot and Spinach Dog Muffins	Beef and Sweet Potato Stew	Turkey and Cranberry Dog Biscuits	Chicken Liver and Pumpkin Bites
9	Blueberry and Banana Frozen Treats	Chicken and Rice Soup	Turkey and Vegetable Stir-Fry	Cheese and Carrot Dog Biscuits
10	Peanut Butter and Banana Bites	Turkey and Vegetable Casserole	Beef and Vegetable Stew	Pumpkin and Oatmeal Dog Treats
11	Apple and Carrot Dog Cookies	Salmon and Sweet Potato Bake	Chicken and Rice Pilaf	Turkey and Cranberry Dog Biscuits
12	Pumpkin and Oatmeal Dog Treats	Beef and Sweet Potato Stew	Chicken and Vegetable Stir-Fry	Chicken Liver and Pumpkin Bites
13	Blueberry and Banana Frozen Treats	Chicken and Rice Soup	Turkey and Vegetable Casserole	Cheese and Carrot Dog Biscuits
14	Carrot and Spinach Dog Muffins	Turkey and Cranberry Dog Biscuits	Beef and Vegetable Stew	Peanut Butter and Banana Bites
15	Chicken Liver and Pumpkin Bites	Salmon and Sweet Potato Bake	Chicken and Rice Pilaf	Apple and Carrot Dog Cookies
16	Cheese and Carrot Dog Biscuits	Beef and Sweet Potato Stew	Turkey and Cranberry Dog Biscuits	Pumpkin and Oatmeal Dog Treats

17	Peanut Butter and Banana Bites	Chicken and Rice Soup	Turkey and Vegetable Stir-Fry	Blueberry and Banana Frozen Treats
18	Apple and Carrot Dog Cookies	Turkey and Vegetable Casserole	Beef and Vegetable Stew	Chicken Liver and Pumpkin Bites
19	Pumpkin and Oatmeal Dog Treats	Salmon and Sweet Potato Bake	Chicken and Rice Pilaf	Cheese and Carrot Dog Biscuits
20	Blueberry and Banana Frozen Treats	Beef and Sweet Potato Stew	Turkey and Cranberry Dog Biscuits	Carrot and Spinach Dog Muffins
21	Chicken Liver and Pumpkin Bites	Chicken and Rice Soup	Turkey and Vegetable Casserole	Peanut Butter and Banana Bites
22	Cheese and Carrot Dog Biscuits	Beef and Vegetable Stew	Chicken and Vegetable Stir-Fry	Apple and Carrot Dog Cookies
23	Carrot and Spinach Dog Muffins	Turkey and Cranberry Dog Biscuits	Beef and Sweet Potato Stew	Pumpkin and Oatmeal Dog Treats
24	Peanut Butter and Banana Bites	Chicken and Rice Pilaf	Turkey and Vegetable Stir-Fry	Blueberry and Banana Frozen Treats
25	Apple and Carrot Dog Cookies	Turkey and Vegetable Casserole	Beef and Vegetable Stew	Chicken Liver and Pumpkin Bites

26	Pumpkin and Oatmeal Dog Treats	Salmon and Sweet Potato Bake	Chicken and Rice Pilaf	Cheese and Carrot Dog Biscuits
27	Blueberry and Banana Frozen Treats	Beef and Sweet Potato Stew	Turkey and Cranberry Dog Biscuits	Carrot and Spinach Dog Muffins
28	Chicken Liver and Pumpkin Bites	Chicken and Rice Soup	Turkey and Vegetable Casserole	Peanut Butter and Banana Bites
29	Cheese and Carrot Dog Biscuits	Beef and Vegetable Stew	Chicken and Vegetable Stir-Fry	Apple and Carrot Dog Cookies
30	Carrot and Spinach Dog Muffins	Turkey and Cranberry Dog Biscuits	Beef and Sweet Potato Stew	Pumpkin and Oatmeal Dog Treats

MEAL PLANNER JOURNAL

Meal Planner

Week of:

Monday	Tuesday	Wednesday
BREAKFAST	BREAKFAST	BREAKFAST
LUNCH	LUNCH	LUNCH
DINNER	DINNER	DINNER
SNACK	SNACK	SNACK

Thursday	Friday	Saturday
BREAKFAST	BREAKFAST	BREAKFAST
LUNCH	LUNCH	LUNCH
DINNER	DINNER	DINNER
SNACK	SNACK	SNACK

Sunday	NOTES:
BREAKFAST	
LUNCH	
DINNER	
SNACK	

Meal Planner

Week of:

Monday	Tuesday	Wednesday
BREAKFAST	BREAKFAST	BREAKFAST
LUNCH	LUNCH	LUNCH
DINNER	DINNER	DINNER
SNACK	SNACK	SNACK

Thursday	Friday	Saturday
BREAKFAST	BREAKFAST	BREAKFAST
LUNCH	LUNCH	LUNCH
DINNER	DINNER	DINNER
SNACK	SNACK	SNACK

Sunday	NOTES:
BREAKFAST	
LUNCH	
DINNER	
SNACK	

Meal Planner

Week of:

Monday	Tuesday	Wednesday
BREAKFAST	BREAKFAST	BREAKFAST
LUNCH	LUNCH	LUNCH
DINNER	DINNER	DINNER
SNACK	SNACK	SNACK

Thursday	Friday	Saturday
BREAKFAST	BREAKFAST	BREAKFAST
LUNCH	LUNCH	LUNCH
DINNER	DINNER	DINNER
SNACK	SNACK	SNACK

Sunday	NOTES:
BREAKFAST	
LUNCH	
DINNER	
SNACK	

Meal Planner

Week of:

Monday		
BREAKFAST		
LUNCH		
DINNER		
SNACK		

Tuesday		
BREAKFAST		
LUNCH		
DINNER		
SNACK		

Wednesday		
BREAKFAST		
LUNCH		
DINNER		
SNACK		

Thursday		
BREAKFAST		
LUNCH		
DINNER		
SNACK		

Friday		
BREAKFAST		
LUNCH		
DINNER		
SNACK		

Saturday		
BREAKFAST		
LUNCH		
DINNER		
SNACK		

Sunday		
BREAKFAST		
LUNCH		
DINNER		
SNACK		

NOTES:

Meal Planner

Week of:

Monday	Tuesday	Wednesday
BREAKFAST	BREAKFAST	BREAKFAST
LUNCH	LUNCH	LUNCH
DINNER	DINNER	DINNER
SNACK	SNACK	SNACK

Thursday	Friday	Saturday
BREAKFAST	BREAKFAST	BREAKFAST
LUNCH	LUNCH	LUNCH
DINNER	DINNER	DINNER
SNACK	SNACK	SNACK

Sunday	NOTES:
BREAKFAST	
LUNCH	
DINNER	
SNACK	

Meal Planner

Week of:

Monday	**Tuesday**	**Wednesday**
BREAKFAST	BREAKFAST	BREAKFAST
LUNCH	LUNCH	LUNCH
DINNER	DINNER	DINNER
SNACK	SNACK	SNACK
Thursday	**Friday**	**Saturday**
BREAKFAST	BREAKFAST	BREAKFAST
LUNCH	LUNCH	LUNCH
DINNER	DINNER	DINNER
SNACK	SNACK	SNACK

Sunday	NOTES:
BREAKFAST	
LUNCH	
DINNER	
SNACK	

Meal Planner

Week of:

Monday	Tuesday	Wednesday
BREAKFAST	BREAKFAST	BREAKFAST
LUNCH	LUNCH	LUNCH
DINNER	DINNER	DINNER
SNACK	SNACK	SNACK

Thursday	Friday	Saturday
BREAKFAST	BREAKFAST	BREAKFAST
LUNCH	LUNCH	LUNCH
DINNER	DINNER	DINNER
SNACK	SNACK	SNACK

Sunday	NOTES:
BREAKFAST	
LUNCH	
DINNER	
SNACK	

Meal Planner

Week of:

Monday	Tuesday	Wednesday
BREAKFAST	BREAKFAST	BREAKFAST
LUNCH	LUNCH	LUNCH
DINNER	DINNER	DINNER
SNACK	SNACK	SNACK

Thursday	Friday	Saturday
BREAKFAST	BREAKFAST	BREAKFAST
LUNCH	LUNCH	LUNCH
DINNER	DINNER	DINNER
SNACK	SNACK	SNACK

Sunday	NOTES:
BREAKFAST	
LUNCH	
DINNER	
SNACK	

Meal Planner

Week of:

Monday	Tuesday	Wednesday
BREAKFAST	BREAKFAST	BREAKFAST
LUNCH	LUNCH	LUNCH
DINNER	DINNER	DINNER
SNACK	SNACK	SNACK

Thursday	Friday	Saturday
BREAKFAST	BREAKFAST	BREAKFAST
LUNCH	LUNCH	LUNCH
DINNER	DINNER	DINNER
SNACK	SNACK	SNACK

Sunday	NOTES:
BREAKFAST	
LUNCH	
DINNER	
SNACK	

Meal Planner

Week of:

Monday	Tuesday	Wednesday
BREAKFAST	BREAKFAST	BREAKFAST
LUNCH	LUNCH	LUNCH
DINNER	DINNER	DINNER
SNACK	SNACK	SNACK

Thursday	Friday	Saturday
BREAKFAST	BREAKFAST	BREAKFAST
LUNCH	LUNCH	LUNCH
DINNER	DINNER	DINNER
SNACK	SNACK	SNACK

Sunday	NOTES:
BREAKFAST	
LUNCH	
DINNER	
SNACK	

Meal Planner

Month of:

Sun	Mon	Tues	Wed	Thurs	Fri	Sat